dreamers

THE GIRL WHO PLAYED WITH NUMBERS

This book belongs to

Read more in the Dreamers series by Lavanya Karthik

Scan QR code to access the
Penguin Random House India website

THE GIRL
WHO PLAYED
WITH NUMBERS

SHAKUNTALA DEVI

Written and illustrated by
LAVANYA KARTHIK

duckbill

An imprint of Penguin Random House

For you, unique number, and the patterns you will make.

DUCKBILL BOOKS

Duckbill Books is an imprint of the Penguin Random House group of companies
whose addresses can be found at global.penguinrandomhouse.com

Published by Penguin Random House India Pvt. Ltd.
4th Floor, Capital Tower 1, MG Road,
Gurugram 122 002, Haryana, India

Penguin
Random House
India

First published in Duckbill Books by
Penguin Random House India 2024

ISBN 9780143464778

Typeset in Georgia by DiTech Publishing Services Pvt. Ltd
Printed at Replika Press Pvt. Ltd, India

www.penguin.co.in

MIX
Paper | Supporting
responsible forestry
FSC
www.fsc.org
FSC™ C016779

'Numbers . . . come to life; they're not just symbols on paper.'

—Shakuntala Devi

Do Numbers scare you?

Does the thought of maths make you tremble at the knees, send chills up your spine?

From the moment Shakuntala Devi met Numbers, they became her closest friends. The most complex maths problems were like games that she played with her friends. She became so good at mental calculations that she was called the Human Computer! But long before she became a legend, she was just a girl with some unusual friends.

This is her story.

I was three when I first met the Numbers.

Appa was in the courtyard of our home in Bangalore, practising a card trick. I watched him shuffle the cards and arrange them in rows.

And there *they* were—peeping out from each card! I watched them hop and skip, form teams and play.

What fun, I thought.
Would they let me play too?

'Shaku, guess where Number 3 is!' Appa said.

'Right here!' I squealed, tapping 3 on her head.

'I bet you can't find 7,' he smiled.

'Just did!' I giggled.

'And 8?'

'Got you!'

Again and again, Appa shuffled and rearranged the cards and challenged me to tell him where a Number was hiding. Again and again, I found them!

'Hmm, you have a good memory,' Appa said. 'But let's see what you can do with bigger numbers.'

He brought a slate and wrote down Numbers, in ones and twos.

Add! Subtract! Multiply! Divide!

The Numbers raced, but I kept up.

Then the Numbers formed larger groups.

Add! Subtract! Multiply! Divide!

They formed patterns and stories.
They whispered their secrets to me.
They invited me into their world.

I jumped right in!

1*1=1

11*11=121

111*111=12321

1111*1111=1234321

11111*11111=123454321

11111 = 41 * 271 * 1

22222 = 41 * 271 * 2

33333 = 41 * 271 * 3

44444 = 41 * 271 * 4

55555 = 41 * 271 * 5

$0 * 9 + 1$

$1 * 9 + 2$

$12 * 9 + 3$

$123 * 9 + 4$

$1234 * 9 + 5$

$12345 * 9 + 6$

$123456 * 9 + 7$

$1234567 * 9 + 8$

I loved Numbers. But sometimes, I longed for other things.

'Won't I learn all this in school?' I asked. 'I want to go outside and play,' I said.

'You don't need school,' Appa said. 'And you certainly don't need play. Now do these sums again.'

I was four when Appa began taking me to schools and colleges to show off my skills. How they stared as I answered their questions, using all the tricks the Numbers had shown me.

'Add 756 to 829.'
Easy!

1585

339624

'Multiply 356 by 954.'
Hah!

679248

'Double that!
Now find its cube root!'

87.904

I did . . . and
did again!

I was six when Appa took me to the University of Mysore. A room full of professors had gathered, waiting to test me.

A child this young!' they scoffed. 'A girl who's never been to school!' They smiled and patted my head.

At first, their questions were simple.

Add! Subtract! Multiply! Divide!

With each answer I gave, their smiles grew smaller.

'Is this a trick?' they asked. 'Is she really calculating these numbers in her mind?'

Then, their questions grew more complicated! The Numbers they threw at me grew larger and larger.

They wanted to scare me with Numbers!

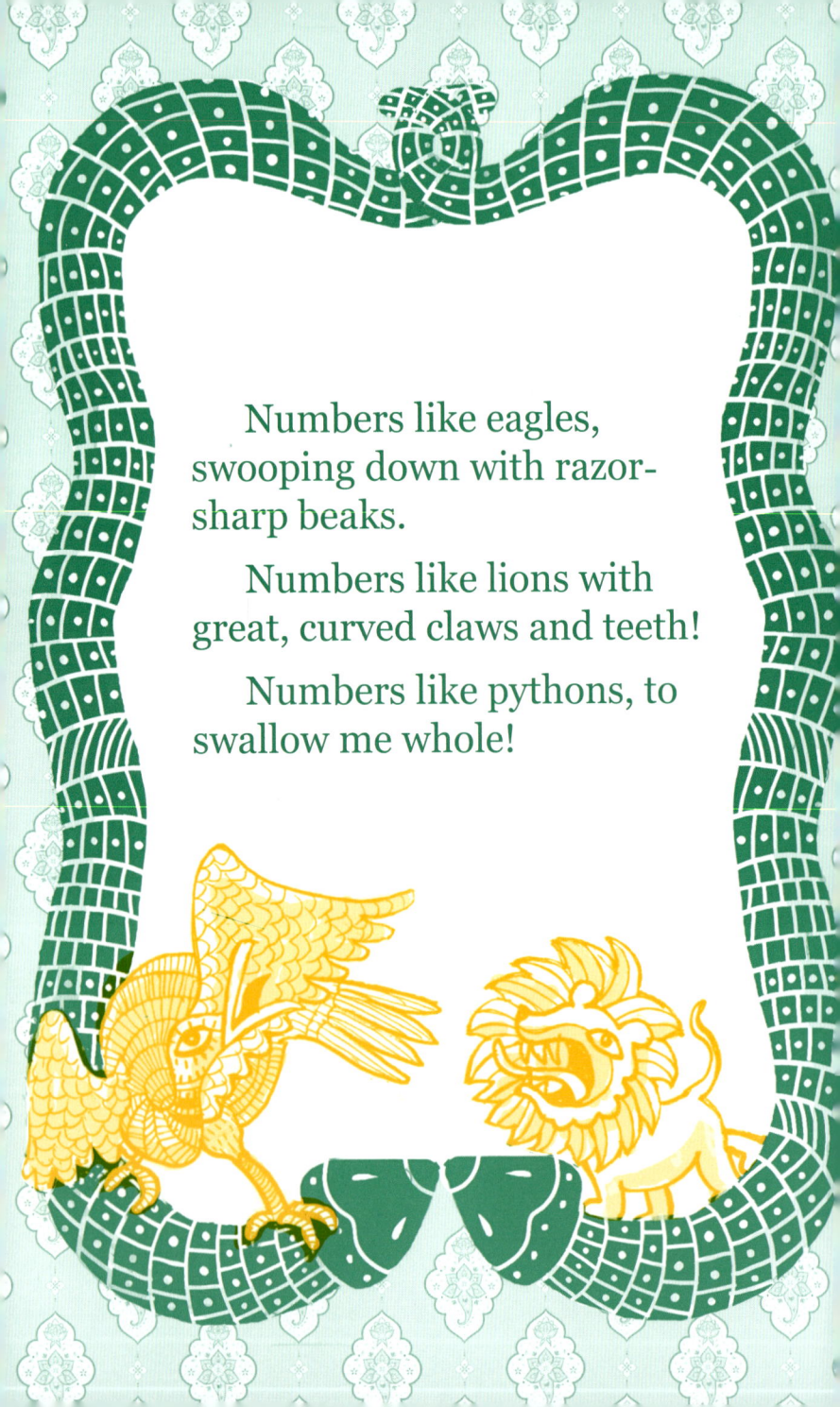

Numbers like eagles, swooping down with razor-sharp beaks.

Numbers like lions with great, curved claws and teeth!

Numbers like pythons, to swallow me whole!

'Let's play!'
I laughed and
jumped right in.

The world of
Numbers was an endless
adventure, a game I
never tired of playing.

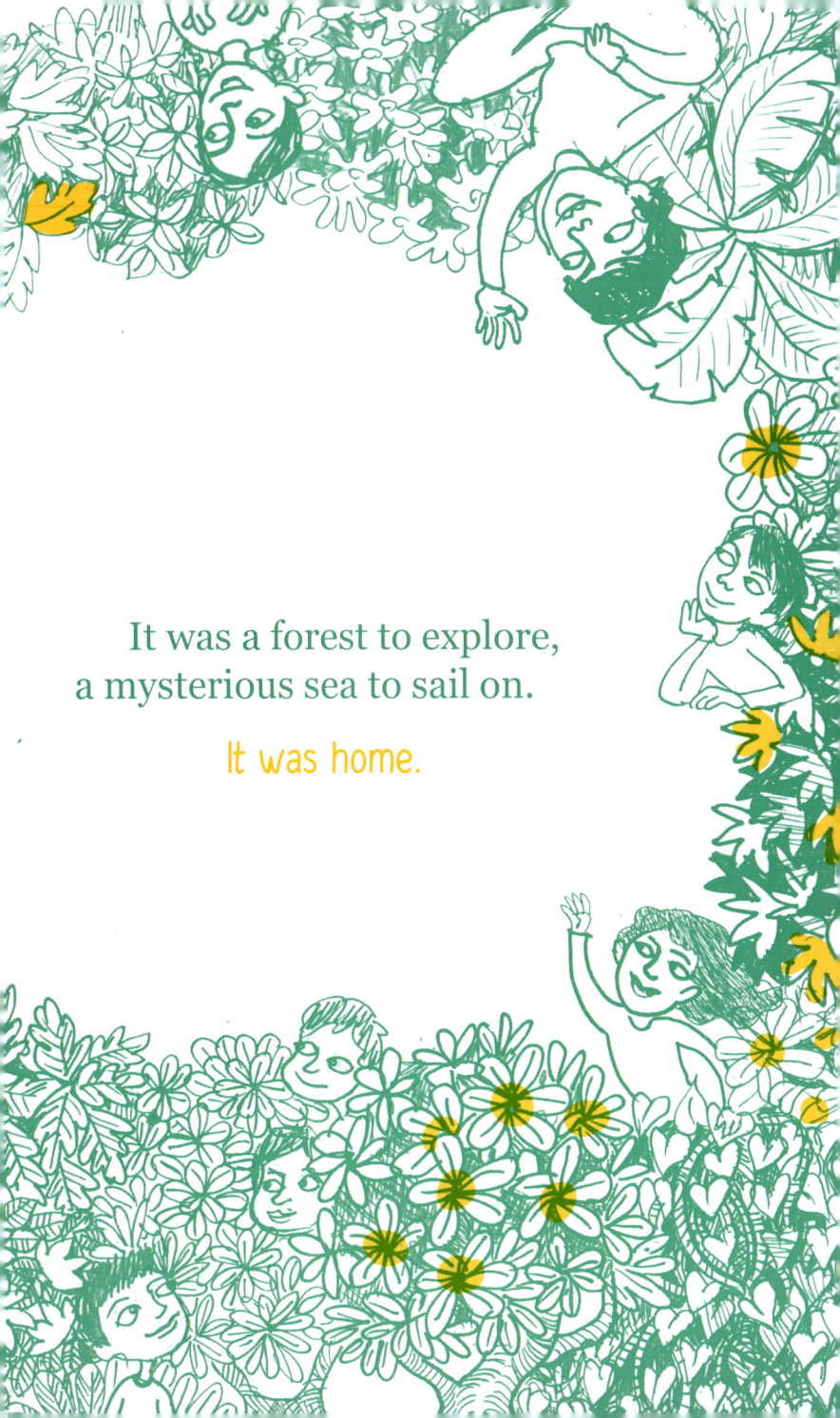

It was a forest to explore,
a mysterious sea to sail on.

It was home.

I was eight and famous.
I did shows before packed
audiences.

I was ten and
travelling to shows in
neighbouring towns.

5 3 1 6 2 7

I was eleven when I realized I was becoming a Number myself.

The number of times my name was mentioned in newspapers.

The number of shows I did in a week.

The number of people paying to watch my shows.

The number of rupees I earned, on which my whole family lived.

6 3 7 2

Were my skills with maths
the only thing people saw in me?
Was that all I was worth?

I felt lonely and sad.

I had no one to turn to or
confide in.

No one, except . . .

Numbers.

They became my comfort when I felt angry and alone.

Numbers were truth when the people around me weren't.

Numbers were joy and wonder when the world seemed grim.

Numbers were the wings that would take me to a future of my making.

I travelled the world on those wings, meeting people of every kind.

I opened the doors to the world of Numbers, to people everywhere.

And at last, I discovered the simplest of truths.

We *are* Numbers. But not the kind that pay bills and grace marksheets.

We are unique numbers, with a value all our own.

We form patterns with others—

Add! Subtract!
Multiply! Divide!

We change as
we grow, and the
patterns we make
together change too.

So the next time you meet a Number that scares you, don't shrink in fear.

Look closely. See its value. Imagine the patterns you could make together and the stories you could be.

Time to play!
Jump right in!

Shakuntala Devi (4 November 1929–
21 April 2013) spent her life sharing her love
for numbers with the world. She wrote many
books that explained the methods she used
for complex calculations, and celebrated the
wonder of maths.

Computers, she said, were just machines.
The human mind was vastly more complex
and anyone could train, like her, to calculate.
All you needed was to make friends with
numbers.

In 1980, at the Imperial College in London,
she mentally calculated the product of two
thirteen-digit numbers in just twenty-eight
seconds. This feat won her a place in the
Guinness Book of World Records.

*The illustrations in this book are inspired
by the Mysore school of painting.*

7686369774870 * 2465099145179
=
18947608127905628462873730

Lavanya Karthik is an author and illustrator by day, a cookie monster by teatime and fast asleep by nine at night. She lives in Mumbai where she eats a lot of chocolates and takes a lot of naps.